itty**bitty**books™

BABY NAMES FOR BOYS

THOMAS NELSON PUBLISHERS
Nashville

Published in Nashville, Tennessee by Thomas Nelson, Publishers and distributed in Canada by Lawson Falle, Ltd., Cambridge, Ontario.

**Library of Congress
Cataloging-in-Publication Data**

Baby names for boys.
      p.   cm—(Itty bitty books)
    ISBN 0-8407-6855-9
    1. Names, Personal—Dictionaries.
  2. Masculine names—Dictionaries.
I. Thomas Nelson Publishers. II. Series:
Itty bitty books.
CS2377.B228 1992
929.4'03—dc20   92-29028
                       CIP

Printed in Singapore.
1 2 3 4 5 6 7 8 — 98 97 96 95 94 93

ABBREVIATIONS

Af.	African	*M.E.*	Middle English
Ar.	Arabic	*Mus.*	Muslim
Aram.	Aramaic	*N.A.*	Native American
Celt.	Celtic	*O.D.*	Old Dutch
Dut.	Dutch	*O.E.*	Old English
Eng.	English	*O.F.*	Old French
Fr.	French	*O.G.*	Old German
Gael.	Gaelic	*O.N.*	Old Norse
Ger.	German	*Pers.*	Persian
Gr.	Greek	*Rus.*	Russian
Heb.	Hebrew	*Scan.*	Scandinavian
Hin.	Hindi	*Sl.*	Slavic
Hun.	Hungarian	*Sp.*	Spanish
In.	Indian	*Wel.*	Welsh
Ir.	Irish		
It.	Italian	*var.*	variation
Jap.	Japanese		
Lat.	Latin		

AARON *Heb.*–enlightened; exalted.
Aharon, Aranne, Ari, Arin, Arnie, Arny, Aron, Arron, Erin, Haroun

ABRAHAM *Heb.*–father of the multitude.
Abe, Abey, Abie, Abram, Abran, Avram, Avrom, Bram, Ibrahim

ADAIR *Gael.*–from the oak tree ford.

ADAM *Heb.*–man of the red earth.
Ad, Adamo, Adams, Adan, Addie, Addy, Ade, Adhamb

ADRIAN *Lat.*–from Adria.
Ade, Adriano, Adrien, Hadrian

AIDAN *Gael.*–fire; warmth of the home.
Aiden

ALAN *Gael.*–handsome; cheerful; peaceful.
Ailin, Al, Alain, Alair, Aland, Alann, Alano, Alanson, Alanus, Allan, Allayne, Allen, Alley, Alleyn, Allie, Allyn, Alon

ALASTAIR *Gael.*–form of Alexander.
Al, Alasdair, Alasteir, Alaster, Alistair, Alister, Allister

ALBERT *O.E.*–highborn; noble and bright.
Adelbert, Ailbert, Al, Alberto,

Albie, Albrecht, Aubert, Bert,
Bertie, Berty, Elbert

ALDEN *O.E.*–old friend.
Al, Aldin, Aldwin, Elden, Eldin

ALEXANDER *Gr.*–helper,
defender of mankind.
Alec, Alejandro, Alejo, Alek,
Aleksandr, Allesandro, Alex,
Alexandr, Alexandre, Alexandro,
Alexandros, Alexio, Alexis, Alic,
Alick

ALFRED *O.E.*–elf counselor; wise
counselor.
Al, Alf, Alfie, Alfredo, Alfy, Avery

ALI *Ar.*–exalted; greatest.
Aly

ALPHONSE *O.G.*–noble and
eager; eager for battle.
*Al, Alf, Alfie, Alfons, Alfonso,
Alfonzo, Alford, Alfy, Alonso,
Alonzo, Alphonso, Fons, Fonsie,
Fonz, Fonzie, Lon, Lonnie*

ALTON *O.E.*–old town.

ALVIN *O.G.*–old or noble friend.
*Al, Aloin, Aluin, Aluino, Alva,
Alvan, Alvie, Alvy, Alvyn, Alwin,
Alwyn, Elvin, Elwin*

AMIEL *Heb.*–lord of my people.

AMOS *Heb.*–borne by God.

ANATOLE *Gr.*–from the east.
Anatol, Anatolio

ANDREW *Gr.*–strong; manly.
Anders, Andie, Andonis, Andre,
Andrea, Andreas, Andrej,
Andres, Andrés, Andrey,
Andrius, Andy

ANGELO *Gr.*–messenger; angel.

ANGUS *Gael.*–unique choice; one
strength.
Ennis, Gus

ANSEL *O.F.*–follower of a
nobleman.
Ancell, Ansell

ANSON *O.G.*–son of divine
origin.
Annson, Hanson

ANTHONY *Lat.*–invaluable; priceless.
Antin, Antoine, Anton, Antone, Antoni, Antonin, Antonino, Antonio, Antonius, Antons, Antony

ARCHIBALD *O.G.*–valorous; bold.
Arch, Archaimbaud, Archambault, Archer, Archibaldo, Archibold, Archie, Archy

ARDEN *Lat.*–ardent, fiery, enthusiastic.

ARIEL *Heb.*–lion of God.

ARISTOTLE *Gr.*–superior; best.

ARLEN *Gael.*–pledge.
Arlan, Arles, Arlin

ARMAND *O.G.*–army man.
Arman, Armando, Armin

ARNOLD *O.G.*–strong as an
eagle; eagle-ruler.
*Arnaldo, Arnaud, Arne, Arney,
Arni, Arnie, Arnoldo, Arny*

ARTHUR *Celt.*–bear; stone.
*Art, Artair, Arte, Arther, Arthor,
Artie, Artur, Arturo, Artus, Arty*

ARVIN *O.E.*–friend of the people;
friend of the army.

ASA *Heb.* physician.

ASHER *Heb.*–happy.

ASHFORD *O.E.*–ash-tree ford.

ASHLEY *O.E.*–ash tree meadow.
Ash, Asheley, Ashlan, Ashlin

AUBREY *O.F.*–elf ruler.
*Alberik, Aube, Auberon, Avery,
Oberon*

AVERILL *M.E.*–April;
boar-warrior.
Ave, Averell, Averil

AXEL *O.G.*–father of peace.
Aksel, Ax, Axe, Axil

BAILEY *O.F.*–bailiff.
Baile, Bailie, Baillie, Baily

BAIRD *Gael.*–balladeer; singer.
Bar, Bard, Barde, Barr

BALDWIN *O.G.*–bold friend.
Bald, Balduin, Baudoin

BARCLAY *O.E.*–birch tree meadow.
Bar, Bark, Barklay, Berkeley, Berkie, Berkley, Berky

BARNABAS *Gr.*–son of comfort or consolation.
Barnaba, Barnabe, Barnaby, Barnebas, Barney, Barnie, Barny, Burnaby, Nab

BARNETT *O.E.*–nobleman.
Barn, Barney, Baronett, Barron

BARRET *O.G.*–strong as a bear.
Bar, Barratt, Barrett, Bear

BARTON *O.E.*–from the barley farm.
Barrton, Bart, Bartie, Barty

BARUCH *Heb.*–blessed.

BASIL *Lat.*–kingly.
Base, Basile, Basilio, Basilius, Vasilis, Vassily

BAXTER *O.E.*–baker.

BEAUMONT *Fr.*–beautiful hill.

BEAUREGARD *O.F.*–beautiful face or expression.
Beau, Bo

BELLAMY *O.F.*–handsome friend.
Belamy, Bell

BENEDICT *Lat.*–blessed.
Ben, Bendick, Bendict, Bendix, Benedetto, Benedick, Benedicto, Benedikt, Bengt, Benito, Bennie, Bennt, Benny, Benoit, Bent

BENJAMIN *Heb.*–son of the right hand.
Ben, Beniamino, Benjamen, Benji, Benjie, Benjy, Benn, Bennie, Benny, Benyamin, Jamie, Jim

BENTON   *O.E.*–moor or coarse grass.

BERNARD   *O.G.*–brave bear.
Barnard, Barney, Barnie, Barny, Bear, Bearnard, Bern, Bernardo, Bernarr, Berne, Bernhard, Bernhardo, Bernie, Berny, Burnard

BERTRAM   *O.E.*–glorious raven.
Bart, Bartram, Beltran, Bert, Bertie, Berton, Bertrand, Bertrando, Berty

BEVAN   *Gael.*–son of Evan.
Bev, Beven, Bevin, Bevon

BJORN   *Scan.*–bear.

BLAINE   *Gael.*–thin, slender.
Blane, Blayne

BLAIR *Gael.*–plain; flat land.

BLAKE *O.E.*–pale and fair.

BOGART *O.F.*–strong as a bow.

BOONE *O.F.*–good.

BOOTH *O.E.*–dwelling place; hut.
Boot, Boote, Boothe

BORDEN *O.E.*–valley of the boar.

BORG *Scan.*–castle.

BORIS *Slav.*–battler, warrior.

BOWIE *Gael.*–blond.
Bow, Bowen, Boyd

BOYCE *O.F.*–woodland.

BRADEN *O.E.*–wide valley.
Bradan, Brade, Bradin

BRADFORD *O.E.*–broad river crossing.

BRADLEY *O.E.*–wide meadow. *Brad, Bradly, Bradney, Lee, Leigh*

BRADSHAW *O.E.*–large forest.

BRADY *O.E.*–broad island.

BRAMWELL *O.E.*–of Abraham's well; where the broom sage grows.

BRANDON *O.E.*–beacon hill. *Bran, Brand, Branden, Brandy, Brandyn, Brannon*

BRENDAN *Gael.*–stinky hair. *Bren, Brenden, Brendin, Brendis, Brendon, Brennan, Brennen, Bryn*

BRENTON   *O.E.*–from the steep hill.
Brent, Brentyn

BRETT   *Celt.*–Briton.
Bret, Bretton, Brit, Britt

BREWSTER   *O.E.*–brewer.

BRIAN   *Gael.*–strength.
*Briano, Briant, Brien, Brion,
Bryan, Bryant, Bryen, Bryon*

BRIGHAM   *O.E.*–enclosed bridge;
village near the bridge.

BROCK   *O.E.*–badger.

BRODERICK   *O.E.*–brother;
broad ridge.
Brod, Broddie, Broddy, Broderic

BRODY *Gael.*–ditch.
Brodee, Brodie

BRONSON *O.E.*–the brown man's son.
Bron, Bronnie, Bronnson, Bronny

BROOK *O.E.*–stream; brook.
Brooke, Brookes, Brooks

BRUCE *O.F.*–brushwood thicket.

BRUNO *It.*–brown-haired or dark-skinned.

BURGESS *O.E.*–citizen, especially of a fortified town.
Burg, Burgiss, Burr

BURKE *O.F.*– fortified settlement.
Berk, Berke, Bourke, Burk

BURNE O.E.–brook; stream.
Bourn, Bourne, Burn, Byrne

BURRIS O.E.–of the town.

BURTON O.E.–fortress.

CAESAR *Lat.*–hairy; emperor.
Casar, Cesar, Cesare, Cesaro,
Kaiser, Seasar

CALDWELL *O.E.*–cold spring.

CALEB *Heb.*–bold one; dog.
Cal, Cale, Kaleb

CALHOUN *Celt.*–narrow woods;
warrior.

CALVERT *O.E.*–herdsman.
Cal, Calbert

CALVIN *Lat.*–bald.
Cal, Calv, Kalvin, Vin, Vennie,
Vinny

CAMDEN *Gael.*–winding valley.

CAMERON   *Gael.*–crooked nose.
Cam, Camey, Cammy

CAMPBELL   *Gael.*–crooked mouth.

CANUTE   *Scan.*–knot.
Cnut, Knut, Knute

CARLETON   *O.E.*–farmer's village.
Carl, Carlton, Charlton

CARLISLE   *O.E.*–fortified town or tower.
Carl, Carlie, Carly, Carlyle

CARMINE   *Lat.*–song.

CARNEY   *Gael.*–victorious; winner.
Car, Carny, Karney, Kearney

CARSON   *O.E.*–son of the marsh dwellers.

CARTER   *O.E.*–cart driver or maker.

CARVER   *O.E.*–woodcarver.

CASEY   *Gael.*–brave.

CASPER   *Pers.*–treasurer or treasure guard.
Caspar, Cass, Cassie, Cassy, Gaspar, Gaspard, Gasparo, Gasper, Jasper, Kaspar, Kasper

CASSIDY   *Gael.*–clever.
Cass, Cassady, Cassie, Cassy

CASSIUS   *Lat.*–vain.

CECIL *Lat.*–blind.
Cece, Cecile, Cecilio, Cecilius, Celio

CEDRIC *O.E.*–war chieftain.
Cad, Caddaric, Ced, Rick, Rickie, Ricky

CHADWICK *O.E.*–soldier's town.

CHAIM *Heb.*–life.
Haim, Hayim, Hy, Hyman, Hymie, Mannie, Manny

CHALMERS *Gael.*–son of the lord.

CHANDLER *O.F.*–candlemaker.
Chan, Chane.

CHANEY *Fr.*–oak tree.
Cheney

CHANNING *O.E.*–knowing.

CHAPMAN *O.E.*–merchant;
peddler.

CHARLES *O.G.*–man; strong.
*Carl, Carlo, Carlos, Carrol,
Carroll, Cary, Caryl, Chad,
Chaddie, Chaddy, Charley,
Charlie, Charlot, Charlton, Chas*

CHAUNCEY *M.E.*–chancellor.
Chan, Chance, Chancey, Chaunce

CHESTER *O.E.*–fortified camp or
town.

CHRISTIAN *Gr.*–follower of Christ.
Chretien, Chris, Chrissie, Chrissy, Christiano, Christie, Christy, Cristian, Kit, Kris, Krispin, Kristian

CHRISTOPHER
Gr.–Christ-bearer.
Christoffer, Christoforo, Christoper, Christoph, Christophe, Christophorus, Cris, Cristobal, Cristoforo, Christos, Kit, Kristo, Kristofer, Kristofor, Kristoforo, Kristos

CLARENCE *Lat.*–bright; famous.
Clair, Clarance, Clare

CLARK O.F.–scholar.
Clarke, Clerc, Clerk

CLAUDE Lat.–lame.
Claudell, Claudian, Claudianus, Claudio, Claudius, Claus

CLAYBORNE O.E.–born of the earth.
Claiborn, Claiborne, Clay, Clayborn, Claybourne

CLAYTON O.E.–farm built on clay.

CLEMENT Lat.–merciful.
Clem, Clemens, Clemente, Clementius, Clemmie, Clemmy, Clim, Klemens, Klement, Kliment

CLEVELAND *O.E.*–cliff or high area.
Cleavland, Cleve, Clevy, Clevie

CLIFFORD *O.E.*–cliff at the river crossing.

CLIFTON *O.E.*–town near the cliffs.

CLINTON *O.E.*–headland farm.

CLYDE *Gael.*–rocky eminence; heard from afar; *Wel.*–warm.

CODY *O.E.*–a cushion or pillow.

COLBERT *O.E.*–outstanding seafarer.
Cole, Colt, Colvert, Culbert

COLBY *O.E.*–dark farm.
Cole

COLEMAN *O.E.*–adherent of Nicholas.
Cole, Colman

COLIN *Gael.*–child; youth.
Cailean, Colan, Cole, Collin

COLLIER *O.E.*–miner.
Colier, Colis, Collayer, Collis, Collyer, Colyer

COLTON *O.E.*–dark village; coal town.

CONLAN *Gael.*–hero.
Con, Conlen, Conley, Conlin, Conn

CONNOR *Gael.*–high desire.

CONRAD *O.G.*–honest or brave counselor.
Conrade, Conrado, Cort, Koenraad, Konrad, Kort, Kurt

CONWAY *Gael.*–holy river.

COOPER *O.E.*–barrelmaker.

CORBETT *Lat.*–raven.
Corbet, Corbie, Corbin, Corby

CORDELL *O.F.*–ropemaker.
Cord, Cordie, Cordy, Cory

CORNELIUS *Lat.*–like a horn.
Conney, Connie, Conny, Cornall, Cornell, Corney, Cornie, Corny, Cory, Neel, Nelly

COSMO *Gr.*–order, harmony, the universe.
Cos, Cosimo, Cosme, Cozmo

COURTLAND *O.E.*–from the farmstead or court land.

COURTNEY *O.F.*–court member.
Cort, Court, Courtnay, Curt

COWAN *Gael.*–hillside hollow.
Coe, Cowey, Cowie

CRAIG *Gael.*–crag; rock.

CRANDALL *O.E.*–the cranes' valley.
Cran, Crandal, Crandell

CRAWFORD *O.E.*–ford of the crows.

CREIGHTON *O.E.*–rocky place.
Creigh, Creight, Crichton

CRISPIN *Lat.*–curly haired.

CROSBY *Scan.*–from or at the shrine of the cross.
Crosbie, Cross

CULLEN *Gael.*–handsome.
Cull, Cullan, Culley, Cullie, Cullin, Cully

CURRAN *Gael.*–hero.

CURTIS *O.F.*–courteous.
Curcio, Curt, Curtice, Kurtis

CYRIL *Gr.*–lordly.
Cirillo, Cirilo, Cy, Cyrill, Cyrille, Cyrillus

CYRUS *Pers.*–sun.

DALE *O.E.*–valley.
Dael, Dal, Dayle

DALLAS *Gael.*–wise; skilled.
Dal, Dall, Dallis

DALTON *O.E.*–the village or
estate in the valley.

DAMIAN *Gr.*–to tame.
*Dame, Damiano, Damien,
Damon*

DANA *Scan.*–from Denmark.
Dane

DANIEL *Heb.*–God is my judge.
*Dan, Dani, Dannial, Danill,
Dannel, Dannie, Danny*

DANTE *Lat.*–lasting; enduring.

DARBY　*Gael.*–free man;
O.N.–from the deer estate.
Dar, Darb, Darbee, Derby

DARCY　*Gael.*–dark; *O.F.*–from
Arcy.
D'Arcy, Dar, Darce

DARIUS　*Gr.*–wealthy.

DARNELL　*O.E.*–hidden place.
Dar, Darn, Darnall

DARREL　*Fr.*–beloved; darling.
*Dare, Darral, Darrell, Darrill,
Darryl, Daryl, Daryle, Derril*

DARREN　*Gael.*–great.
*Dare, Daren, Darin, Daron,
Darrin, Darron, Derron*

DARWIN *O.E.*–dear friend.
Derwin, Derwynn

DAVID *Heb.*–beloved.
*Dav, Dave, Davey, Davidde,
Davide, Davidson, Davie, Davin,
Davis, Daven, Davon, Davy, Dov*

DAVIS *O.E.*–son of David.

DEAN *O.E.*–valley.
Deane, Dene, Deyn, Dino

DELANEY *Gael.*–child of the
challenger.
Delainey, Delany

DELBERT *O.E.*–bright as day.
Bert, Bertie, Berty, Dalbert, Del

DEMETRIUS   *Gr.*–following
Demeter.
Demetre, Demetri, Demetris,
Dimitri, Dimitry, Dmitri

DEMPSEY   *Gael.*–proud.

DENNIS   *Gr.*–of Dionysus.
Den, Denis, Dennet, Denney,
Dennie, Dennison, Denny, Denys,
Dion, Dionisio, Dionysus, Ennis

DENVER   *O.E.*–green valley.

DEREK   *O.G.*–rule of the people.
Darrick, Deric, Derick, Derrek,
Derrick, Derrik, Derk, Dirk

DERRY   *Gael.*–red-haired; from
Derry.

DESMOND *Gael.*–man from south Munster.
Des, Desi, Desmund

DEVIN *Gael.*–poet.
Dev, Devon, Devy

DEVLIN *Gael.*–brave; fierce.
Dev, Devland, Devlen

DEWEY *Wel.*–prized. Var. of David.

DOMINIC *Lat.*–belonging to the Lord.
Dom, Domenic, Domenico, Domingo, Dominick, Dominik, Dominique, Nick, Nickie, Nicky

DONALD *Gael.*–world ruler; world power.
Don, Donal, Donall, Donalt, Donaugh, Donn, Donnell, Donnie, Donny

DONNELLY *Gael.*–brave, brown-haired man.
Don, Donn, Donnell, Donnie, Donny

DONOVAN *Gael.*–dark warrior.
Don, Donavon, Donn, Donnie, Donny

DOUGLAS *Gael.*–black water.
Doug, Dougie, Douglass, Dougy, Dugaid

DOVEV *Heb.*–to whisper.
Dov

DOYLE *Gael.*–dark stranger.

DRAKE *M.E.*–owner of the Sign of the Dragon inn.

DREW *O.F.*–sturdy; *Wel.*–wise.
Dru, Drud, Drugi

DUANE *Gael.*–little and dark; swarthy.
Dewain, Dwain, Dwayne

DUNCAN *Gael.*–dark-skinned fighter.

DUNHAM *Celt.*–dark man.

DUSTIN *O.G.*–brave fighter.
Dust, Dustan, Dustie, Duston

DYLAN *Wel.*–from the sea.
Dilan, Dill, Dillie, Dilly

EARL *O.E.–nobleman.*
Earle, Earlie, Early, Erl, Erle,
Errol, Erroll, Erryl, Rollo

EDGAR *O.E.–rich spearman.*
Ed, Eddie, Eddy, Edgard,
Edgardo

EDMUND *O.E.–rich protector.*
Eadmund, Eamon, Ed, Edd,
Eddie, Edmon, Edmond,
Edmondo, Ned

EDWARD *O.E.–happy or wealthy*
protector.
Ed, Eddie, Eddy, Edik, Edouard,
Eduard, Eduardo, Edvard, Ewart

EDWIN *O.E.–rich friend.*
Eadwinn, Ed, Eddie, Eddy, Edlin,
Eduino, Lalo, Ned, Neddie, Neddy

ELIJAH   *Heb.*–Jehovah is God.
El, Eli, Elia, Elias, Elihu, Aliot,
Elliott, Ellis, Ely, Elyott

ELLERY   *O.E.*–elder tree island.
Ellary, Ellerey

ELLSWORTH   *O.E.*–nobleman's
estate.
Ellswerth, Elsworth

ELTON   *O.E.*–old town.
Alden, Aldon, Eldon

ELVIS   *Scan.*–all wise.
Al, Alvis, Alvys, El

ELWOOD   *O.E.*–from the old
wood.

EMERSON   *O.G.*–son of the
industrious ruler.

EMERY *O.G.*–industrious ruler.
Amerigo, Amery, Amory,
Emmerich, Emmerie, Emmery,
Emory

EMIL *Lat.*–flattering, winning.
Emelen, Emile, Emilio, Emlen,
Emlyn

EMMANUEL *Heb.*–God is with
us.
Eman, Emanuel, Emanuele,
Immanuel, Mannie, Manny,
Manuel.

ENGELBERT *O.G.*–bright as an
angel.
Bert, Bertie, Berty, Englebert,
Ingelbert, Inglebert

EPHRAIM   *Heb.*–fruitful; productive.
Efrem, Efren, Ephrem

ERIC   *Scan.*–all ruler; ever-powerful.
Erek, Erich, Erick, Erik, Errick, Eryk, Rick, Rickie, Ricky

ERNEST   *O.E.*–earnest; sincere.
Ernesto, Ernestus, Ernie, Ernst, Erny

ETHAN   *Heb.*–firm.

EUGENE   *Gr.*–well-born.
Eugen, Eugene, Eugenio, Eugenius, Gene

EVAN *Wel.*–young warrior. Var. of John.

Ev, Even, Evin, Evyn, Ewan, Ewen, Owen

FABIAN *Lat.*–bean grower.
*Fabe, Fabek, Faber, Fabert,
Fabiano, Fabien, Fabio*

FALKNER *O.E.*–falconer.
Faulkner, Fowler

FARRELL *Gael.*–hero.
Farr, Farrel, Ferrel, Ferrell

FELIX *Lat.*–fortunate.
*Fee, Felic, Felice, Felicio, Felike,
Feliks, Felizio*

FELTON *O.E.*–village or camp on
the meadow.

FENTON *O.E.*–marshland farm.

FERDINAND *O.G.*–daring
voyager.
*Ferd, Ferdie, Ferdo, Ferdy,
Fergus, Fernando, Hernando*

FERGUS *Gael.*–supreme choice.
Fearghas, Fergie, Ferguson

FERRIS *Gael.*–var. of Peter, the rock.
Farris, Ferriss

FIDEL *Lat.*–faithful.
Fidele, Fidelio

FINLAY *Gael.*–little fair-haired soldier.
Fin, Findlay, Findley, Finley, Finn

FITZGERALD *O.E.*–son of the spear ruler.
Fitz, Gerald, Gerrie, Gerry, Jerry

FITZPATRICK *O.E.*–son of a nobleman.

FLEMING *O.E.*–a Dutchman.
Flem, Flimming

FLETCHER *M.E.*–arrow-featherer,
fletcher.
Flecber, Fletch

FLYNN *Gael.*–son of the
red-haired man.

FORBES *Gael.*–field.

FOREST, FORREST *O.F.*–forest;
woodsman.
*Forester, Forrester, Forster, Foss,
Foster*

FOWLER *O.E.*–trapper of wild
fowl.

FRANCIS *Lat.*–a Frenchman.
Cbico, Fran, Francesco,

Franchot, Francisco, Franciskus,
Francois, Frank, Frankie,
Franky, Frannie, Franny, Frans,
Fransisco, Frants

FRANKLIN   *M.E.*–free landowner.
Fran, Francklin, Francklyn,
Frank, Frankie, Franklyn,
Franky

FRAZER   *O.E.*–curly-haired.
Fraser, Frasier, Fraze, Frazier

FREDERICK   *O.G.*–peaceful
ruler.
Eric, Erich, Erick, Erik, Federico,
Fred, Freddie, Freddy, Fredek,
Frederic, Frederich, Frederico,
Frederigo, Frederik, Fredric,
Fredrick, Friedrich, Friedrick

FREEMAN *O.E.*–free man.
Free, Freedman, Freeland,
Freemon

FREMONT *O.G.*–guardian of
freedom.

FULBRIGHT *O.G.*–very bright.
Fulbert, Philbert

FULLER *O.E.*–one who shrinks
cloth.

FULTON *O.E.*–a field near the
town.

GABRIEL *Heb.*–hero of God.
*Gabbie, Gabby, Gabe, Gabi,
Gabie, Gabriele, Gabriello, Gaby,
Gavriel*

GALEN *Gael.*–healer; calm.
Gaelan, Gale, Gayle

GANNON *Gael.*–fair-skinned.

GARDNER *M.E.*–gardener.
*Gar, Gard, Gardener, Gardie,
Gardiner, Gardy*

GARETH *Wel.*–gentle.
Gar, Garth

GARFIELD *O.E.*–spear field.

GARLAND *O.E.*–from the
battlefield; *O.F.*–wreath.

GARNER *O.F.*–armed sentry; grain gatherer.

GARRICK *O.E.*–spear-rule.
Garek, Garik, Garrek, Garrik

GARVEY *Gael.*–rough peace.

GARY *O.E.*–spear.
Gare, Garey, Garry

GAVIN *Wel.*–white hawk.
Gav, Gavan, Gaven, Gawain, Gawen

GEORGE *Gr.*–farmer.
Egor, Georas, Geordie, Georg, Georges, Georgie, Georgy, Giorgio, Goran, Jorgan, Jorge Yurik

GERALD *O.G.*–spearruler.
Egor, Garald, Garold, Gary, Gearalt, Gearard, Gerard, Gerek, Gerick, Gerik, Gerrard, Gerri, Gerrie, Gerry, Giraldo, Giraud, Jerald, Jerrie, Jerrold, Jerry, Jorgen, Jurek, Yurik, Ygor

GIDEON *Heb.*–feller of trees; destroyer.

GILBERT *O.E.*–trusted; bright pledge.
Gilberto, Gilburt, Gill, Giselbert, Guilbert, Wilbert, Wilbur, Wilburt, Will

GILROY *Gael.*–devoted to the red-haired man.
Gil, Gildray, Gill, Gillie, Gilly, Roy

GLENDON   *Gael.*–village in the valley.
Glen, Glenden, Glenn

GODDARD   *O.G.*–divinely firm.
Godard, Godart, Goddart, Godhart, Gothart, Gotthardt

GORDON   *O.E.*–hill on the meadows or plains.
Gordan, Gorden, Gordie, Gordy

GRADY   *Gael.*–noble, illustrious.
Gradiegh, Gradey

GRAHAM   *O.E.*–the gray home.
Graehme, Graeme, Gram

GRANGER   *O.E.*–farmer.

GRANT *Fr.*–tall; great.
Grantham, Granthem, Grantley, Grenville

GRANTLAND *O.E.*–great plains.

GREGORY *Lat.*–watchman; watchful.
Graig, Greg, Gregg, Greggory, Gregoire, Gregoor, Gregor, Gregorio, Gregorious

GRIFFITH *Wel.*–fierce chief; ruddy.

GROVER *O.E.*–from the grove.

GUTHRIE *Gael.*–from the windy place; *O.G.*–war hero.
Guthrey, Guthry

GUY   *Fr.*–guide; *O.G.*–warrior.
Guido

HADLEY *O.E.*–from the heath.
*Had, Hadlee, Hadleigh, Lee,
Leigh*

HALDAN *Scan.*–half-Danish.
Hal, Halden, Halfdan, Halvdan

HALEY *Gael.*–ingenious; hay
meadow.
*Hailey, Haily, Hal, Hale, Haliegh,
Lee, Leigh*

HALSEY *O.E.*–from Hal's island.

HAMID *Ar.*–thanking God.

HAMILTON *O.E.*–proud or
beloved estate.

HANLEY *O.E.*–high meadow.
*Hanlea, Hanleigh, Henleigh,
Henley*

HARDY   *O.G.*–bold; brave, daring.

HARLAN   *O.E.*–from the army land.
Harland, Harlen, Harlin

HARLEY   *O.E.*–from the long field.
Arley

HARLOW   *O.E.*–from the rough hill or army-hill.
Arlo

HAROLD   *Scan.*–army-ruler.
Araldo, Hal, Harald, Haroldas, Harry, Herold, Herrick

HARPER   *O.E.*–harp player.

HARTLEY   *O.E.*–deer meadow.

HARVEY *O.G.*–strong and ardent.
Harv, Herve, Hervey

HASIN *In.*–laughing.
Hasen, Hassin

HASKEL *Heb.*–understanding and intellect.
Haskell

HASTINGS *O.E.*–son of the stern man.

HAVELOCK *Scan.*–sea battle.

HAYDEN *O.E.*–from the hedged valley.
Haydon

HAYES *O.E.*–from the hedged place.

HEATH *M.E.*–from the heath.

HENRY *O.G.*–ruler of an estate.
*Arrigo, Enrico, Enrique, Hal,
Hank, Harry, Heike, Heindrick,
Heinrich, Heinrik, Hendrick,
Hendrik, Henri, Henrik*

HILARY *Lat.*–cheerful.
*Hi, Hilaire, Hilario, Hilarius,
Hill, Hillary, Hillery, Hillie, Hilly,
Ilario*

HILLEL *Heb.*–greatly praised.

HILTON *O.E.*–town on the hill.

HOGAN *Gael.*–youth.

HOLBROOK *O.E.*–brook near
the hollow.
Brook, Holbrooke

HOLDEN *O.E.*–the hollow in the valley.

HOLLIS *O.E.*–grove of holly trees.

HOLMES *M.E.*–from the river islands.

HOLT *O.E.*–woods; forest.

HORTON *O.E.*–from the gray estate.
Hort, Horten, Orton

HOUSTON *O.E.*–hill town.

HOWARD *O.E.*–watchman.

HUGH *O.E.*–intelligence.

HUMPHREY *O.G.*–peaceful Hun.
*Hum, Humfrey, Humfrid,
Humfried, Hump, Humph,*

Hunfredo, Onfre, Onfroi,
Onofredo

HUNTER *O.E.*–hunter.

HUNTINGTON *O.E.*–hunting
estate.
Hunt, Huntingdon

HUNTLEY *O.E.*–hunter's
meadow.
Hunt, Huntlee, Lee, Leigh

HUSSEIN *Ar.*–little and
handsome.
Husain, Husein

HUTTON *O.E.*–the house on the
bluff.

HUXLEY *O.E.*–Hugh's meadow.

IAN *Gael.*–var. of John.
Iain

INGEMAR *Scan.*–famous son;
Ing's son.
Ingamar, Ingmar

INGRAM *O.E.*–angel; raven.
Inglis, Ingram, Ingrim

INNIS *Gael.*–island.
Innes, Inness

IRA *Heb.*–watchful.

IRVING *Gael.*–beautiful; *O.E.*–sea
friend.
*Earvin, Erv, Ervin, Erwin, Irv,
Irvin, Irvine, Irwin, Irwinn*

ISAAC *Heb.*–he laughs; laughter.
*Ike, Ikey, Isaak, Isac, Isacco,
Isak, Itzak, Izaak, Izak*

ISIDORE *Gr.*–gift of Isis.
*Dore, Dory, Isador, Isadore,
Isidor, Isidoro, Isidro, Izzy*

ISRAEL *Heb.*–ruling with the
Lord; wrestling with the Lord.

IVAN *Rus.*–var of John.

IVAR *Scan.*–archer.
Ive, Iver, Ivor, Yvon, Yvor

JACOB *Heb.*–supplanter.
*Giacobo, Giacomo, Giacopo,
Hamish, Iago, Jack, Jackie,
Jacky, Jacobo, Jacques, Jaime,
Jake, Jakie*

JAMAL *Ar.*–beauty; handsome.
Jamaal, Jammal

JAMES *Eng.*–var. of Jacob.
*Diego, Giacomo, Giamo,
Hamish, Iago, Jacques, Jaime,
Jameson, Jamesy, Jamey, Jamie,
Jamison, Jay, Jayme, Jim,
Jimmie, Jimmy, Seamus, Seumas,
Shamus*

JARED *Heb.*–to descend.
*Jarad, Jarid, Jarrad, Jarred,
Jarrett, Jarrid, Jarrod, Jerad*

JARVIS *O.G.*–keen with a spear.

JASON *Gr.*–healer.
Jaisen, Jase, Jasen, Jasun, Jay, Jayson

JEDIDIAH *Heb.*–beloved of the Lord.

JEFFERSON *O.E.*–son of Jeffrey.

JEFFREY *O.F.*–heavenly peace.
Geoff, Geoffrey, Godfrey, Gottfried, Jeff, Jefferey, Jeffie, Jeffy, Jeffry

JEREMIAH *Heb.*–Jehovah exalts.
Dermot, Diarmid, Geremia, Jere, Jereme, Jeremias, Jeremy, Jerry

JEROME *Lat.*–holy name.
Gerome, Gerrie, Gerry,

Hieronymus, Jere, Jereme,
Jerrome, Jerry

JESSE *Heb.*–God exists.
Jess, Jessee, Jessey, Jessie

JESUS *Heb.*–God will help; God
will save.
Chucho, Jecho

JOACHIM *Heb.*–the Lord will
judge.
Akim, Joaquin

JOEL *Heb.*–Jehovah is the Lord.

JOHN *Heb.*–God is gracious.
Evan, Ewan, Ewen, Gian,
Giavani, Giovanni, Hana, Hans,
Iain, Ian, Jack, Jackie, Jacky,
Jan, Janos, Jean, Jens, Jock,

Jocko, Johan, Johann, Johannes,
Johnnie, Johnny, Johny, Jon, Jone,
Juan, Owen, Sean, Shaughn,
Shaun, Shawn, Zane

JONATHAN   *Heb.*–Jehovah gave;
God's gift.
Jonathan, Johnathon, Jon,
Jonathon, Yanaton

JORDAN   *Heb.*–descend.
Giordano, Jared, Jerad, Jordon,
Jory, Jourdain

JOSEPH   *Heb.*–God shall add or
increase.
Che, Giuseppe, Iosep, Jo, Joe,
Joey, Jose, Jozef

JOSHUA   *Heb.*–Jehovah saves.
Josh, Joshia, Joshuah

JUDE *Lat.*–right in the law; praise.

JULIAN *Lat.*–belonging or related to Julius.
Julien

JULIUS *Gr.*–youthful.
Giulio, Jolyon, Jule, Jules, Julie, Julio

JUSTIN *Lat.*–upright; fair.
Giustino, Guisto, Justen, Gustinian, Justino, Justis, Justus

KAREEM *Ar.*–noble, generous.
Karim

KEANE *O.E.*–sharp, keen.
Kean, Keen, Keene

KEEFE *Gael.*–cherished;
handsome.

KEEGAN *Gael.*–small and fiery.

KEENAN *Gael.*–small and
ancient.

KEIR *Celt.*–dark-skinned.
Kerr

KEITH *Wel.*–from the forest;
Gael.–from the battle place.

KELLY *Gael.*–warrior.
Kele, Kellen, Kelley

KELSEY *Scan.*–from the ship
island.

KELTON *O.E.*–keel town; town
where ships are built.
Keldon, Kelson

KELVIN *O.E.*–lover of ships.
Kelwin

KENDALL *O.E.*–from the bright
valley; from the valley of the Kent
river.
*Ken, Kendal, Kendell, Kenn,
Kennie, Kenny*

KENDRICK *Gael.*–son of Henry;
O.E.–royal ruler.

KENLEY *O.E.*–from the king's meadow.
Kenleigh

KENNEDY *Gael.*–helmeted chief.
Canaday, Ken, Kenn, Kennie, Kenny

KENNETH *Gael.*–handsome.
Kennet, Kennith

KENYON *Gael.*–white-haired; blond.

KERRY *Gael.*–dark; dark-haired.
Keary

KERWIN *O.E.*–friend of the marshlands.

KEVIN *Gael.*–gentle, lovable, handsome.
Kev, Kevan, Keven, Kevon

KIERAN *Gael.*–small and dark-skinned.
Kiernan

KILLIAN *Gael.*–small and warlike.
Kilian, Killie, Killy

KIMBALL *O.E.*–warrior chief; bold ruler.
Kim, Kimbell, Kimble

KINCAID *Celt.*–battle chief.

KINGSLEY *O.E.*–from the king's meadow.
King, Kingsly, Kinsley

KINGSTON *O.E.*–from the king's estate.

KIRBY *Scan.*–church village.
Kerby

KIRK *Scan.*–church.
Kerk

KNOX *O.E.*–from the hills.

KWASI *Af.*–born on Sunday.

KYLE *Gael.*–handsome; from the strait.
Kiel, Kile, Kiley, Ky, Kylie

LAMAR *O.G.*–famous throughout the land; famous as the land.
Lemar

LAMBERT *O.G.*–bright land; bright as the land.
Bert, Bertie, Berty, Lamberto, Landbert

LAMONT *Scan.*–lawyer.
Lammond, Lamond, Monty

LANCE *O.G.*–servant.
Lancelot, Launce

LANE *M.E.*–narrow road.
Laney, Lanie

LANGDON *O.E.*–from the long hill.
Landon, Langsdon, Langston

LANGLEY   *O.E.*–from the long meadow.

LATHAM   *Scan.*–from the barn.

LAWFORD   *O.E.*–a ford on the hill.

LAWRENCE   *Lat.*–from Laurentium; laurel-crowned.
Larry, Lars, Lauren, Laurence, Laurens, Laurent, Laurie, Lauritz, Lawry, Lenci, Lon, Lonnie, Lonny, Lornat, Loren, Lorens, Lorenzo

LAWTON   *O.E.*–from the town on the hill.
Laughton, Law

LEIF   *Scan.*–beloved.

LEIGHTON *O.E.*–from the meadow village.
Lay, Layton

LELAND *O.E.*–meadow land.
Lee, Lealand, Leeland, Leigh

LEONARD *O.G.*–bold lion.
Lee, Len, Lenard, Lennard, Lennie, Lenny, Leo, Leon, Leonardo, Leonerd, Leonhard, Leonid, Leonidas, Lonnard, Lonnie, Lonny

LEROY *O.F.*–king.
Elroy, Lee, Leigh, Leroi, LeRoy, Roy

LESLIE *Gael.*–from the gray castle.
Lee, Leigh, Les, Lesley, Lezlie

LESTER *Lat.*–from the chosen camp; *O.E.*–from Leicester.
Leicester, Les

LEVI *Heb.*–joined.
Levey, Levin, Levon, Levy

LINCOLN *O.E.*–from the town by the pool.

LINDSAY *O.E.*–linden tree island.
Lind, Lindsey

LIONEL *O.F.*–lion cub.

LIVINGSTON *O.E.*–Leif's town.

LLEWELLYN *Wel.*–lionlike; lightning.
Lew, Lewis, Llywellyn

LLOYD *Wel.*–gray-haired.
Floyd, Loy, Loydie

LOGAN *Gael.*–from the small hollow.

LOUIS *O.G.*–renowned warrior.
Aloysius, Lew, Lewis, Lou, Louie, Lucho, Ludvig, Ludwig, Luigi, Luis

LOWELL *O.F.*–little wolf.
Lovell, Loew

LUCIAN *Lat.*–shining, light.
Luciano, Lucien

LUCIUS *Lat.*–bringer of light; *Gr.*–from Lucanus.
Luca, Lucais, Lucas, Luce, Lucias, Lucio, Lukas, Luke

LUTHER   *O.G.*–famous warrior.
Lothaire, Lothario, Lutero

LYLE   *O.F.*–from the island.
Lisle, Ly, Lyell

LYNDON   *O.E.*–from the linden
tree hill.
Lin, Lindon, Lindy, Lyn, Lynn

MACKENZIE *Gael.*–son of the wise leader.

MADISON *O.E.*–son of the powerful warrior.

MALCOLM *Gael.*–follower of St. Columba.

MALIK *Mus.*–master.

MALLORY *O.G.*–army counselor; *O.F.*–unhappy.

MARCEL *Lat.*–little and warlike.
Marcello, Marcellus, Marcelo

MARK *Lat.*–warlike.
Marc, Marcos, Marcus, Mario, Marius, Markos, Markus

MARLON O.F.–little falcon.
Marlin

MARLOW O.E.–the hill by the lake.
Mar, Marlo, Marlowe

MARSHALL O.F.–steward; horse-keeper.

MARTIN Lat.–warlike.
Mart, Martainn, Marten, Martie, Martijn, Martino, Marty, Martyn

MARVIN O.E.–lover of the sea.
Maru, Marve, Marven, Marwin, Mervin, Merwin, Merwyn, Murvyn

MASON O.F.–stoneworker.

MATTHEW *Heb.*–gift of the Lord.
Mata, Mateo, Mathe, Mathew,
Mathian, Mathias, Matias, Matt,
Matteo, Matthaeus, Matthaus,
Mattheus, Matthias, Matthieu,
Matthiew, Mattias, Mattie, Matty

MAURICE *Lat.*–dark-skinned.
Mauricio, Maurie, Maurise,
Marits, Maurizio, Maury, Morey,
Morie, Moritz, Morris

MAXWELL *O.E.*–large well; the
important man's well.

MAYNARD *O.G.*–powerful,
strong.
May, Mayne, Menard

MELBOURNE *O.E.*–mill stream.
Mel, Melborn, Melburn

MELVILLE *O.E./O.F.*–town of the hard worker.

MELVIN *Gael.*–polished chief.
Mal, Malvin, Mel, Melvyn, Vin, Vinnie, Vinny

MEREDITH *Wel.*–guardian from the sea; great ruler.
Merideth, Merry

MERLIN *M.E.*–falcon.
Marlin, Marlon, Merle

MERRILL *O.E.*–famous.
Merill, Merle, Merrel, Merrell, Meryl

MERTON *O.E.*–from the town by the sea.
Merv, Merwyn, Murton

MEYER *Ger.*–farmer;
Heb.–bringer of light.
Meier, Meir, Myer

MICHAEL *Heb.*–who is like the
Lord?
*Micah, Michail, Michal, Michale,
Micheal, Micheil, Michel, Michele,
Mickey, Mickie, Micky, Miguel,
Mikael, Mike, Mikel, Mikey,
Mikkel, Mikol, Mishca, Mitch,
Mitchel, Mitchell, Mychal*

MILES *Lat.*–soldier;
O.G.–merciful.
Milo, Myles

MILTON *O.E.*–from the mill
town.

MONROE   *Gael.*–mouth of the Roe River.
Monro, Munro, Munroe

MONTAGUE   *Fr.*–from the pointed mountain.

MONTGOMERY   *O.E.*–from the rich man's mountain.
Monte, Monty

MORGAN   *Gael.*–bright; white; from the edge of the sea.
Morgen, Morgun

MORTON   *O.E.*–town near the moor.
Morten

MUHAMMAD *Ar.*–praised.
Hamid, Hammad, Mahmoud,
Mahmud, Mohammed

MURDOCK *Gael.*–sailor.
Murdoch

MURRAY *Gael.*–sailor.
Morey, Murry

MYRON *Gr.*–fragrant ointment.

NAPOLEON   *Gr.*–lion of the woodland dell; *It.*–from Naples.

NATHANIEL   *Heb.*–gift of God.
Nat, Nataniel, Nate, Nathan, Nathanael, Nathanial, Natty

NEIL   *Gael.*–champion.
Neal, Neale, Neall, Nealon, Neel, Neill, Neils, Nels, Nial, Niall, Niel, Niels, Nil, Niles, Nils

NEVILLE   *O.F.*–new town.
Nev, Nevil, Nevile

NEVIN   *Gael.*–worshipper of the saint; *O.E.*–nephew.
Nefen, Nev, Nevins, Niven

NEWTON   *O.E.*–new town.

NICHOLAS *Gr.*–victory of the people.
Klaus, Niccolo, Nichole, Nichols, Nick, Nickey, Nickie, Nickolas, Nickolaus, Nicky, Nicol, Nicolai

NIGEL *Gael.*–champion.

NOAH *Heb.*–wandering; rest.

NOBLE *Lat.*–well-born.

NOEL *Fr.*–the Nativity; born at Christmas.
Natal, Natale, Nowell

NOLAN *Gael.*–famous; noble.
Noland

NORMAN *O.F.*–Norseman; northerner.
Norm, Normand, Normie, Normy

NORRIS *O.F.*–man from the north; nurse.

NORTHROP *O.E.*–northern farm.
North, Northrup

NORTON *O.E.*–northern town.

OAKLEY *O.E.*–from the oak-tree field.
Oak, Oakes, Oakie, Oakleigh, Oaks

ODELL *Scan.*–little and wealthy.

OGDEN *O.E.*–oak valley or hill.
Ogdan, Ogdon

OLIVER *Lat.*–olive tree; *Scan.*–kind, affectionate.
Noll, Nollie, Nolly, Olivero, Olivier, Oliviero, Ollie, Olly, Olvan

OMAR *Ar.*–first son; highest; follower of the Prophet.

OREN *Heb.*–pine tree;
Gael.–pale-skinned.
Oran, Orin, Oren, Orrin

ORLAND/ORLANDO
O.E.–from the famous land.
Land, Lannie, Lanny, Orlan

ORSON *Lat.*–bearlike.

OSBORN *O.E.*–warrior of God;
Scan.–divine bear.
Osborne, Osbourn, Osbourne

OSMOND *O.E.*–divine protector.
Esme, Osmund, Ozzie, Ozzy

OTTO *O.G.*–rich
Odo, Othello, Otho

PAGE *Fr.*–youthful assistant.
Padget, Padgett, Paige

PALMER *O.E.*–palm-bearer.

PARKER *M.E.*–guardian of the
park.

PARRISH *M.E.*–from the
churchyard.

PASCAL *It.*–pertaining to Easter
or Passover; born at Easter or
Passover.
Pascale, Pace, Pasquale, Patsy

PATRICK *Lat.*–nobleman.
*Paddey, Paddie, Paddy, Padraic,
Padraig, Padriac, Pat, Patton,
Patric, Patrice, Patricio, Patrizio*

PATTON *O.E.*–from the warrior's estate or town.
Pat, Paten, Patin, Paton, Patten

PAUL *Lat.*–small.
Pablo, Pall, Paolo, Paulie, Pauly, Pavel, Poul

PAXTON *Lat.*–from the peaceful town.
Packston, Paxon

PERCIVAL *O.F.*–pierce the valley
Parsifal, Perceval, Percy, Purcell

PERRY *M.E.*–pear tree; *O.F.*–little Peter.

PETER *Gr.*–rock.
Farris, Ferris, Parry, Peadar, Pearce, Peder, Pedro, Peirce,

Perkin, Perren, Perry, Pete,
Peterus, Petey, Petr, Pierce,
Pierre, Pierson, Pieter, Pietrek,
Pietro, Piotr

PEYTON *O.E.*–from the warrior's estate.
Pate, Payton

PHILIP/PHILLIP *Gr.*–lover of horses.
Felipe, Filip, Filippo, Phil,
Philipp, Phillipe, Phillipp,
Pippo

PORTER *Lat.*–gatekeeper.

POWELL *Celt.*–alert.

PRENTICE *M.E.*–apprentice.
Pren, Prent, Prentiss

PRESCOTT *O.E.*–from the priest's cottage.

PRESTON *O.E.*–from the priest's estate.

PRICE *Wel.*–son of the ardent one; Rhys' son.
Brice, Bryce, Pryce

PUTNAM *O.E.*–dweller by the pond.

QUENTIN *Lat.*–fifth; fifth child. *Quent, Quinn, Quint, Quintin, Quinton, Quintus*

QUILLAN *Gael.*–cub.

QUINCY *O.F.*–from the fifth son's estate.

QUINLAN *Gael.*–physically strong.

RADCLIFFE *O.E.*–red cliff.

RAFFERTY *Gael.*–rich and prosperous.
Rafe, Raff, Raffarty

RAFI *Ar.*–exalting.
Raffi, Raffin

RALEIGH *O.E.*–from the red deer meadow.
Lee, Leigh, Rawley

RALPH *O.E.*–wolf-counselor.
Rafe, Raff, Ralf, Raoul, Rolf, Rolph

RAMSAY *O.E.*–from the ram's island; from the raven's island.
Ram, Ramsey

RANCE *Af.*–borrowed all.

RANDOLPH   *O.E.–shield-wolf.*
Rand, Randal, Randall, Randell,
Randolf, Randy

RANSOM   *O.E.–son of the shield.*

RAPHAEL   *Heb.–God has healed.*
Falito, Rafael, Rafaelle, Rafaello

RAVI   *Hin.–sun.*
Ravid, Raviv

RAYBURN   *O.E.–from the deer*
brook.

RAYMOND   *O.E.–mighty or wise*
protector.
Raimondo, Raimund,
Raimundo, Ramon, Ray,
Raymund, Raemonn

RAYNOR *Scan.*–mighty army.
Ragnar, Rainer, Ray, Rayner

REDFORD *O.E.*–from the red
river crossing.

REECE *Wel.*–enthusiastic; fiery.
Rees, Resse, Rhys, Rice

REED *O.E.*–red-haired.
Read, Reade, Reid

REGAN *Gael.*–little king.
Reagan, Reagen, Regen

REGINALD *O.E.*–powerful and
mighty.
*Reg, Reggie, Reggis, Reginauld,
Reinald, Reinaldo, Reinaldos,
Reinbold, Herinold, Renwald,*

Renault, Rene, Reynold, Reynolds, Rinaldo

REMINGTON *O.E.*–from the raven estate.

REUBEN *Heb.*–behold, a son. *Reuven, Rouvin, Rube, Ruben, Rubin, Ruby*

REX *Lat.*–king.

RICHARD *O.G.*–powerful ruler. *Dick, Dickie, Dicky, Ric, Ricard, Ricardo, Riccardo, Rich, Richardo, Richart, Richie, Richy, Rick, Rickard, Rickert, Rickey, Ricki, Rickie, Ricky, Rico, Riki, Riocard*

RICHMOND *O.G.*–powerful
protector.

RIDER *O.E.*–horseman.
Rydder, Ryder

RILEY *Gael.*–valiant.
Reilly, Ryley

RIORDAN *Gael.*–bard, royal
poet.

RIPLEY *O.E.*–from the shouter's
meadow.

ROARKE *Gael.*–famous ruler.
Rorke, Rourke

ROBERT *O.E.*–bright fame.
*Bob, Bobbie, Bobby, Rab,
Riobard, Rip, Rob, Robb, Robbie,*

Robby, Robers, Roberto, Robin,
Rupert, Ruperto, Ruprecht

ROCKWELL   *O.E.*–from the
rocky spring.

RODERICK   *O.G.*–famous ruler.
Roderic, Roderich, Roderigo,
Rodrick, Rodrigo, Rodrique,
Rory, Rurik, Ruy

RODNEY   *O.E.*–island near the
clearing.

ROGER   *O.G.*–famous spearman.
Rodge, Rodger, Rog, Rogerio,
Rogers, Rudiger, Ruggiero,
Rutger, Ruttger

ROLAND *O.G.*–from the famous land.
Lannie, Lanny, Rolando, Roldan, Roley, Rolland, Rollie, Rollin, Rollins, Rollo, Rowland

RONALD *O.E.*–powerful counsel.
Ranald, Ron, Ronnie, Ronny

ROONEY *Gael.*–red-haired.
Rowan, Rowen, Rowney

ROOSEVELT *O.D.*–from the rose field.

RORY *Gael.*–red king.

ROSS *O.F.*–red; *Gael.*–headland.

ROY *O.F.*–king.
Roi, Ruy

RUDYARD   *O.E.*–from the red enclosure.

RUSSELL   *Fr.*–red-haired; fox-colored.

RUTHERFORD   *O.E.*–from the cattle ford.

RUTLEDGE   *O.E.*–from the red pool.

RYAN   *Gael.*–little king.
Ryon, Ryun

SALVATORE *It.*–savior.
Sal, Sallie, Sally, Salvador,
Salvidor, Sauveur, Xaviero,
Zaviero

SAMUEL *Heb.*–told by or asked of
God.
Sam, Sammie, Sammy, Samuele,
Shem

SANBORN *O.E.*–from the sandy
brook.

SANDERS *M.E.*–son of Alexander.
Sander, Sanderson, Sandor,
Sandy, Saunders, Saunderson

SANFORD *O.E.*–sandy river
crossing.

SHERBORN *O.E.*–from the clear brook.
Sherborne, Sherburn, Sherburne

SHERIDAN *Gael.*–wild man.

SHERLOCK *O.E.*–fair-haired.
Sherlocke, Shurlock, Shurlocke

SHERMAN *O.E.*–shearer.

SIDNEY *O.F.*–from St. Denis.
Sid, Sidnee, Syd, Sydney

SIMON *Heb.*–he who hears.
Si, Sim, Simeon, Simmonds, Simone, Syman, Symon

SINCLAIR *O.F.*–from St. Clair.
Clair, Clare, Sinclare

SLOAN *Gael.*–warrior.

SOLOMON *Heb.*–peaceful.

SOMERSET *O.E.*–summer settlement.

SPENCER *M.E.*–dispenser of provisions.
Spence, Spense, Spenser

STAFFORD *O.E.*–riverbank landing place.
Staffard, Staford

STANFORD *O.E.*–from the rocky ford.
Ford, Stan, Standford, Stanfield

STANLEY *O.E.*–from the rocky meadow.
Stan, Stanleigh, Stanly